Dedicated to Ernie, who told me to keep it simple

Simple Studies
for Beginner Brass

for all treble clef brass instruments

John Miller

Faber Music Limited
London

Preface

Simple Studies for Beginner Brass is a comprehensive study course for the early stages of brass playing. The studies are arranged progressively, and each one poses a fresh challenge. My aim has been to cover the entire spectrum of basic technique, including the development of range, stamina and breath control, but at the same time to avoid mere technicalities, since musical abilities must surely grow hand in hand with technical skills. The studies' titles point towards distinct musical styles.

 Simple Studies can be used by any brass player who reads from the treble clef – that is, by players of trumpet, cornet, soprano cornet, flugelhorn, french horn, tenor horn, trombone, baritone, euphornium and bass.

John Miller

JOHN MILLER is one of Britain's leading brass players. He freelanced extensively in London, notably with the London Sinfonietta and the Philip Jones Brass Ensemble, before joining the Philharmonia Orchestra in 1976. He has an international reputation, performing, recording and broadcasting all over the world. In addition to his orchestral work he is a founder member of Equale Brass and a professor of trumpet at the Guildhall School of Music and Drama, London.

© 1987 by Faber Music Ltd
First published in 1987 by Faber Music Ltd
3 Queen Square London WC1N 3AU
Music drawn by Lincoln Castle Music
Cover illustration by Debbie Hinks
Cover design by M & S Tucker
Printed in England by Caligraving Ltd

Contents

Simple Studies for Beginner Brass

John Miller

1. Keep It Simple

2. March

3. Hungarian Hoe-down

4. Pastorale

5. Chinese Dragon

6. Velocity

7. Scots Mist

8. See-saw

9. Pond Life

10. The Long and the Short of It

11. Russian Dance

12. Norwegian Funeral

13. Tip-toe Toccata

14. Supersonic Samurai

15. The Elk's Lament

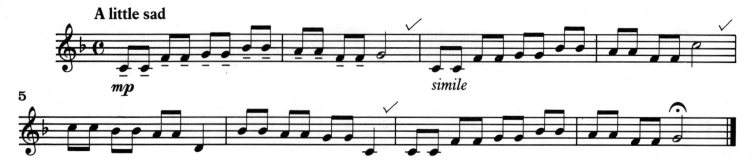

16. Sabre Dance

17. Sombre Song

18. Talisker Isle

19. Bulgarian Dance

20. Firth of Forth

* $\left(\frac{1}{2}\right)$ or (2) for French horn

21. Scottish Warrior

Fierce

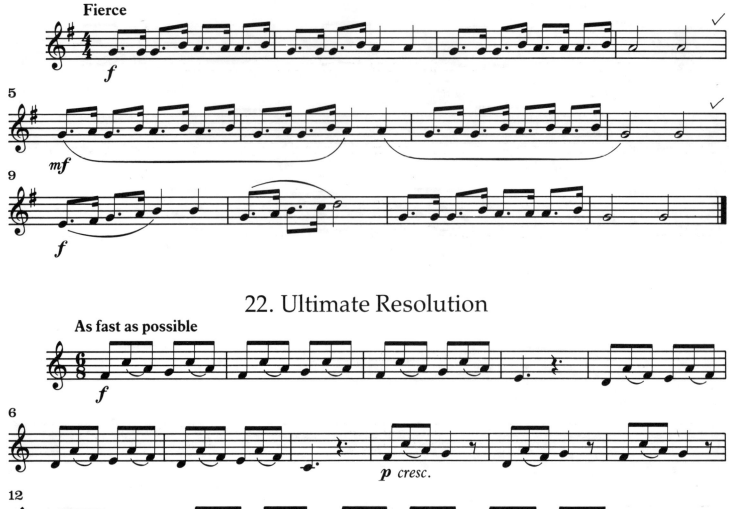

22. Ultimate Resolution

As fast as possible

23. Pink Dream

Not too slow

24. Finger-lickin' Good

25. Nobilmente

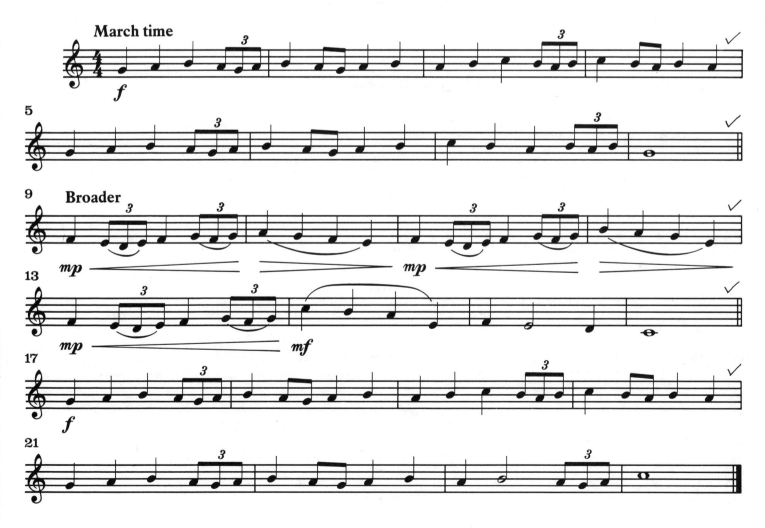

26. Tritone

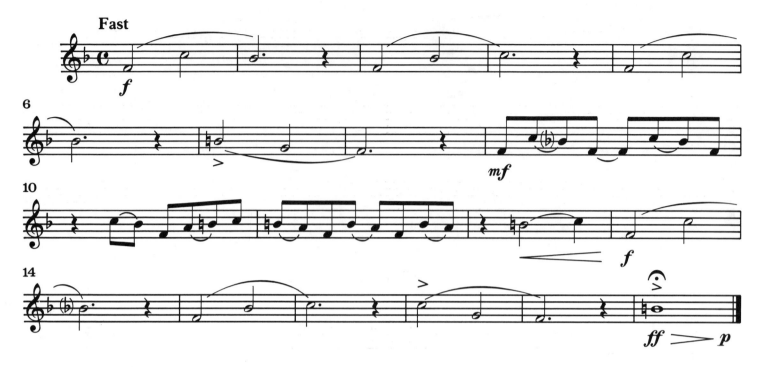

27. Rubic Rumba

28. Perfect Peace

29. Mason's Mazurka

30. Cross Rhythms

* (2) for French horn

3 Nov 98

31. The Easy Easy Winners

32. Contrasts

33. Density 0.3

* (½) for French horn
+ (0) for French horn

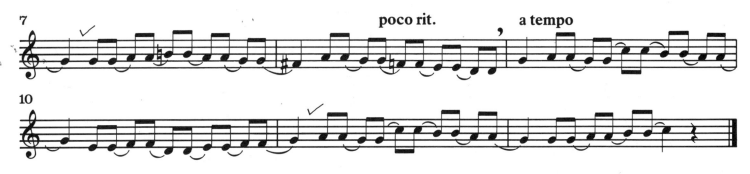

34. Rainy Day

35. The Ilford Intellectual

14

36. Walk Before You Run?

37. Mr. Wimbush

38. Wide Horizon

Printed by J. B. Offset (Marks Tey) Limited, Colchester, Essex.